Read for a Better World™

I0878822

GIGANTORAPTOR

A First Look

TOM JACKSON

Lerner Publications ◆ Minneapolis

Educator Toolbox

Reading books is a great way for kids to express what they're interested in. Before reading this title, ask the reader these questions:

> What do you think this book is about? Look at the cover for clues.
>
> What do you already know about this dinosaur?
>
> What do you want to learn about this dinosaur?

Let's Read Together

Encourage the reader to use the pictures to understand the text.

Point out when the reader successfully sounds out a word.

Praise the reader for recognizing sight words such as *has* and *it*.

TABLE OF CONTENTS

Gigantoraptor 4

You Connect! 21
STEM Snapshot. 22
Photo Glossary 23
Learn More 23
Index 24

Gigantoraptor

Gigantoraptor was a type of dinosaur. It lived ninety-six million years ago.

Gigantoraptor
jy-GAN-tuh-rap-tuh

The dinosaur looked like an ostrich. It was very tall.

What other animals run fast?

It had two legs.
It ran very fast.

The dinosaur had short arms and a long tail.

It may have had long feathers.

How could feathers be helpful?

It had a colorful crest on its head.
Its mouth was a sharp beak.

crest
beak
tail
feathers

Gigantoraptor ate fruits and insects.

The dinosaur laid eggs in a nest. It kept them safe.

What other animals lay eggs?

The dinosaur is
not alive today.
But people
find its bones.

The bones tell us how the dinosaur lived.

You Connect!

What is something you like about this dinosaur?

What else is as big as this dinosaur?

What other dinosaurs do you know about?

STEM Snapshot

Encourage students to think and ask questions like scientists. Ask the reader:

What is something you learned about this dinosaur?

What is something you noticed in the pictures of the dinosaur?

What is something you still don't know about this dinosaur?

Photo Glossary

beak

crest

feather

insect

Learn More

Davis, Bela. *I'm Thinking of a Dinosaur*. Minneapolis: Abdo Kids, 2025.

Hulick, Kathryn. *Dinosaurs*. Minneapolis: Abdo Reference, 2023.

Jones, Christianne C. *Dinosaur Tall and Dinosaur Small: Finding Opposites at the Museum*. North Mankato, MN: Pebble, Capstone, 2025.

Index

beak, 12
eggs, 16–17
feathers, 11
legs, 9
ostrich, 7
tail, 10

Photo Acknowledgments

The images in this book are used with the permission of: © Kostiantyn Ivanyshen/Shutterstock Images, pp. 5, 8, 23 (feathers); © Michael Rosskothen/Shutterstock Images, p. 6; © KensCanning/Shutterstock Images, p. 7; © Elena Duvernay/Dreamstime.com, p. 10; © Crudelitas/Dreamstime.com, p. 11; © Marie Sprunger/Dreamstime.com, pp. 12, 13, 23 (beak), 23 (crest); © Mr1805/Dreamstime.com, pp. 14–15; © Elenarts/Shutterstock Images, pp. 16–17, 18; © Kenneth Carpenter/Wikimedia Commons, p. 20; dwikiyosi01/Shutterstock Images, p. 23 (insect).

Cover Photograph: © Elenarts/Shutterstock Images

Design Elements: © Mighty Media, Inc.

Lerner Publications Company
An imprint of Lerner Publishing Group, Inc.
241 First Avenue North
Minneapolis, MN 55401 USA

For reading levels and more information, look up this title at www.lernerbooks.com.

Main body text set in Mikado a Medium.
Typeface provided by Hannes von Doehren.

Library of Congress Cataloging-in-Publication Data

Names: Jackson, Tom, 1972–author
Title: Gigantoraptor : a first look / Tom Jackson.
Description: Minneapolis : Lerner Publications, [2026] | Series: Read about dinosaurs | Includes bibliographical references and index. | Audience: Ages 5–8 | Audience: Grades K–1 | Summary: "The gigantoraptor was a bird-like dinosaur that we can compare to today's ostrich. Interesting text and realistic images bring this fast and fierce looking dino to life"—Provided by publisher.
Identifiers: LCCN 2025013369 (print) | LCCN 2025013370 (ebook) | ISBN 9798765689813 library binding | ISBN 9798348029074 paperback | ISBN 9798765697702 epub
Subjects: LCSH: Gigantoraptor—Juvenile literature
Classification: LCC QE862.S3 J3286 2026 (print) | LCC QE862.S3 (ebook) | DDC 567.912–dc23/eng/20250728

LC record available at https://lccn.loc.gov/2025013369
LC ebook record available at https://lccn.loc.gov/2025013370

Manufactured in the United States of America
1 - CG - 12/15/25